Democracy in Britain

How citizens can influence decision-making thro

C000109827

Written by Christopher Yeates

Illustrated by Zoe Sadler

Note to teachers:

The content of this book expands and elaborates on the themes presented in the Key Stage 2 series by the same author. In some places the text and accompanying illustrations from the Key Stage 2 books are reproduced here verbatim, or in very similar form.

© Gresham Books 2017
Published by Gresham Books Limited
The Carriage House, Ningwood Manor, Ningwood,
Isle of Wight PO30 4NJ
ISBN 978-0-946095-87-2

Printed in Great Britain

CONTENTS

BRITISH VALUES

Britain is made up of England, Wales and Scotland, and the people who live in these countries are called British. The people of Northern Ireland may also call themselves British and together we make up the United Kingdom. This book is to help you learn about and come to understand some of the British Values we all share.

INTRODUCTION

Critical thinking – how to read this book

In this book you will be asked to debate and evaluate situations and then decide what you think. When you debate, evaluate and decide, you are using your powers of critical thinking.

Learning to become a strong critical thinker will help you think clearly and rationally about what to believe, say, write and do.

The processes of critical thinking provide you with a series of steps to help you analyse, evaluate, debate and decide what you think about situations or choices for yourself.

Step 1: Analyse

What are the facts of the situation or choice?
How do you know the facts are true? Is there any evidence? Is the evidence trustworthy?

Step 2: Debate

Consider all points of view – especially if you disagree – and let everyone have their say. Do you have reasons to support your views? Is there evidence to support your point of view or that of others? Do you think this evidence is strong or weak?

Step 3: Keep an open mind

Are you being open-minded? Are you prepared to listen to the reasons of others and change your mind if their reasons are persuasive? Being prepared to be open-minded is an essential part of becoming a strong critical thinker.

Be honest with yourself. Check for prejudice. Are you being prejudiced? Are others being prejudiced?

Step 4: Evaluate

What are the strengths and weaknesses of the arguments behind each point of view? How strong is the evidence supporting these arguments?

Step 5: Decide

Reflecting on every point of view, and the reasons and evidence you have heard, decide what you think.

To double-check whether you have genuinely been open-minded, ask yourself:

- What is the strongest reason supporting your decision?

- What single piece of evidence helped you decide?

- What reason or piece of evidence might change your mind?

What we mean when we say...

Evaluate: identify the strengths and weaknesses.

Analyse: examine something in detail.

Evidence: facts provided to help prove something is true or false.

Prejudice: a preconceived opinion that is not based on facts or personal experience.

CHAPTER 1: INDIVIDUAL LIBERTY

Democracy is based on the idea of *freedom*. Being free means that you can act, speak, and think however you like – as long as you are not hurting anybody else. You are allowed to make your own choices, and live your life as you wish. In the UK, we call this freedom *individual liberty*. So, an individual (that's you) can do whatever they like, as long as they are not breaking the *rule of law*.

Laws are rules that we all agree to live by, so that society works well for everyone. Laws work in a similar way to school rules. Having rules might feel a bit dull sometimes; but if they are good rules, they can end up giving you more freedom than if they weren't there. For example, it is because of laws that you can go to school, safely practise any religious faith and, when you are older, live with whoever you choose. It is also because of laws that we live in a society that punishes people who break the law and hurt people. The laws in our country apply to everybody.

This all makes a lot of sense, if you think about it, and probably seems quite obvious. Of course you can make your own decisions, and of course if someone breaks the law they get punished. But to most of the humans who have ever lived, these things were not obvious at all. They were not obvious to them because they did not live in democracies, and because they did not have *Human Rights*.

Human Rights are the basic rights every person has simply because they are human; they are the basic things that human beings need in order to live happy and full lives. As a Briton, you have had Human Rights ever since you were born. Human Rights say that everybody is equal. *Equality* is the idea that nobody should be treated differently because of who they are. It is because of Human Rights that you have individual liberty.

In the UK our Human Rights must always be respected, but sadly, there are still many parts of the world where this is not the case.

Some Human Rights you'll be glad to know you have:

- You have the Right to be alive

- You have the Right to be safe from harm

- You have the Right to practise any faith

- You have the Right to speak freely

- Nobody is allowed to torture you

- Nobody is allowed to make you their slave

- Nobody is allowed to treat you as unequal
  and don't let anybody tell you otherwise!

What we mean when we say...

Law: rules we all agree to live by so that society runs well. If a person breaks a law, they are likely to be punished.

Freedom: being able to act, speak and think as you please while still obeying the law.

Human Rights: privileges everybody should have because they are human.

Individual Liberty: being free to enjoy your Human Rights.

Equality: making sure that everybody gets the same opportunity to make the most of their lives and talents.

Debate and evaluate:

In a group, discuss:

1 Look at the list of Human Rights on page 7 and discuss which Human Rights you benefit from every day. In what ways do you think these rights help improve your lives?

2 Do you think that people should be able to speak freely about any topic even if other people find it upsetting? Remember to give reasons for your ideas.

3 Can you think of any laws that help you? How would your life be different without these laws?

Read, research and decide:

1 Explain in your own words what individual liberty means to you.

2 Carry out your own research on equality in Britain. Using evidence from your research write a paragraph answering one of the following questions:

- In Britain today, do you think people with disabilities have the same opportunities as able bodied people?
- Do you believe that men and women are treated equally?
- Do you think it is right to punish people who break laws?

Give reasons to support your ideas.

CHAPTER 2: POLITICS

Politics is the name we use to describe the activities of the people who run – or govern – the country and there are a number of different ways in which a country can be run.

Here in the UK, we run the country using a system called *democracy*. In a democracy, all of the people have a voice in saying how the country is governed. But for a democracy to work well everyone has to get involved and use their voice to talk about the things that matter to them.

To help us organise our democracy, we have a *Parliament* and we have a *Government*.

Parliament makes laws and decides how the country should spend its money, and looks very carefully at the activities of the Government to make sure the Government is doing its job properly.

The Government is the group of people who actually govern, or run, the country and is led by the Prime Minister. For a democracy to work at its best it is very important for people to have their say by voting in a General Election for the people they want to run our country.

What we mean when we say...

Politics: the activities of the people who run the country.

Parliament: the institution that makes laws for the country, agrees taxes and scrutinises the activities of the Government.

Government: the group of people that we have chosen to run our country.

Debate and evaluate:

A democracy works at its best when everyone gets involved and uses their voice to talk about the things that matter to them.

In a group, discuss:

1   Discuss what issues you care about and make a list of three issues that you would like our Government to improve.

2   How well does democracy work in your school? Do you have the opportunity to put your views forward?

Read, research and decide:

1   The head of the Government is the Prime Minister. Carry out your own research and write a paragraph explaining whether you think Britain's Prime Minister is doing a good job. Remember to use evidence from your research to support your views.

2   Imagine you are Prime Minister. Write a short speech explaining three ways that you would like to improve life in Britain.

CHAPTER 3: A BRIEF HISTORY OF DEMOCRACY

The system of democracy began to be used around 2500 years ago in Ancient Greece, as a way of organising how great cities like Athens were run. The first clue is in the name. If we break up the word 'demo-cracy' it means 'rule of the people' in Ancient Greek.

The Athenians introduced the world to *direct democracy*. In this system, every time an important decision had to be made, every free man in the city would gather together, discuss the issue, and *vote*. A vote is a formal expression of your opinion on an important issue, and is a very important part of any democracy. The Athenians used stones to vote; nowadays, as you'll find out later, we use pen and paper, or sometimes a show of hands. In a way, every Athenian *citizen* was a politician, because every citizen was involved in politics: how the city was run.

Notice, however, that only every *free man* in the city was allowed to vote. Women, children, slaves and people not born in Athens were not classed as citizens, and were not allowed to vote. They had very little individual liberty and certainly did not have the kind of Human Rights that we take for granted.

For their time, Athenian ideas about democracy were considered very advanced. Compared to today, however, the way Athenian democracy excluded most of society seems quite primitive, or basic. Still, it was an excellent start, because their idea that lots of people sharing power is better than a few people telling everybody else what to do has become the world's main political system.

Today, even governments that are not democratic sometimes pretend that they are, because they want to be seen to be encouraging Human Rights, even if they are not.

Democracy is the world's main political system. But it isn't the only one. Below are some other ways that countries have been run, or are run today. See what you think:

- **Monarchy:** rule by kings and queens.

- **Dictatorship:** rule by a single individual.

- **Communism:** everything is owned and run by the community.

- **Oligarchy:** rule by a small group of powerful people.

- **Theocracy:** rule by religious authority.

- **Anarchy:** anything goes! Oddly, not as fun as it sounds... can you think why?

What we mean when we say...

Citizen: a legally-recognised member of a country, who has rights.

Direct Democracy: where citizens are directly involved in all political decisions.

Vote: a formal expression of your opinion on something.

Debate and evaluate:

In a group, discuss:

1 Each of the different political systems listed on page 12 has strengths and weaknesses. Make a list of advantages and disadvantages of the following political systems:
   - Dictatorship
   - Communism
   - Theocracy

2 Ancient Athenians used to discuss important issues and hear different points of view before voting on the issue. Discuss the strengths and weaknesses of the following proposals and then vote to decide whether your group would accept or reject them:
   - The school day should start at 11am and finish at 6pm.
   - School uniforms should be the same for boys and girls.
   - Sport should be optional not compulsory.

Read, research and decide:

1 Write a paragraph explaining why you think Ancient Athenians found it helpful to discuss issues and hear more than one point of view before voting.

2 In Ancient Athens free men were allowed to vote but women and slaves were not. Imagine you are a free man in Ancient Athens.

   a) Write three reasons supporting your views that women and slaves should not be allowed to vote. Underline your strongest and most important reason.

   b) Now write three reasons to persuade the free men of Ancient Athens that they should allow women and slaves to be able to vote. Underline your strongest and most important reason.

CHAPTER 4: DEMOCRACY IN THE UK

For a long time, this country was ruled by the *monarchy*. A monarchy is where a King or Queen is Head of State. Monarchs are not *elected*, which means they are not voted for by people like you and me. In the past the King or Queen was all-powerful and made all the laws themselves. This type of monarchy is called *absolute monarchy*, because the monarch had absolute power. Henry VIII is a good example.

Today, we still have a monarch. But our monarch does not 'rule' the country like Henry VIII did, and is not all-powerful. In fact, as we will see, our monarch only plays a small part in the law-making process. The King or Queen is our symbolic leader, but it is Parliament that actually runs the country. This type of 'hands-off' monarchy is called *constitutional monarchy*. But how did we go from a non-democratic, absolute monarchy to a democratic Parliament?

The answer is: very slowly. The first big step was all the way back in 1215, when barons made King John (sworn enemy of Robin Hood) sign an important document called *Magna Carta*. This document said that the King had to obey the law – though, of course, he still made the laws. The second big step was in 1688 and 1689 when, following the Glorious Revolution, another very important document, the *Bill of Rights*, took away a lot of the monarchy's power and gave it to Parliament.

The Bill of Rights was a big step forward for democracy, because it introduced ideas like *elections*, and freedom of speech, a basic Human Right. But it was very limited because Parliament was run by the *aristocracy* – basically, rich men who owned property.

It took another two and a half centuries for women and the working classes to fight successfully for new laws (or Acts) to let them vote in elections. Being able to vote in elections is called *suffrage*. It is only because people used their voices to stand up for *equality* that our Parliament today is truly democratic.

In 1928, a full 239 years after the Bill of Rights, the *Equal Franchise Act* was passed, giving the same voting rights to everybody. When you are 18 years old, you will be able to vote in elections, and use your voice to help decide how the country is run.

What we mean when we say...

Absolute Monarch: a King or Queen who has unlimited political power. There is no Parliament, and therefore no democracy.

Constitutional Monarch: a King or Queen who has very limited political power. The country is run by a democratic Parliament.

Election: an organised choice that is decided by vote.

Act: short for Act of Parliament – another word for law.

Suffrage: the right to vote in an election.

Aristocracy: the highest class in certain societies.

Debate and evaluate:

In a group, discuss:

1 Do you think your school operates like a monarchy or a democracy? Provide at least three specific examples to support your views.

2 Should the voting age be reduced from 18 to 16 years old? Give three reasons for and three against this proposal.

Read, research and decide:

1 Write a paragraph explaining the difference between an absolute monarchy and a constitutional monarchy.

2 Would you prefer to be governed by an absolute or a constitutional monarchy? Give three reasons to support your views.

3 Carry out your own research on the events of either:
   - The Glorious Revolution in 1688
     OR
   - The Equal Suffrage Act in 1928

   Explain why you think either event is so important to the development of democracy in Britain.

CHAPTER 5: DEMOCRACY IN ACTION

Parliament makes laws and we call it the *legislature*. Government uses these laws to run the country so we call it the *executive*.

So, Parliament, also called the *legislature*, makes Britain's laws. The legislature is broken down into three sections: The House of Commons, The House of Lords, and our Constitutional Monarch. You can think of it like a jigsaw, with three pieces coming together to organise our democracy. The biggest and most powerful piece of the jigsaw is the House of Commons, because that is the piece that we, the people, have voted for in elections.

Through *Parliamentary* democracy we elect people to represent us and make decisions on our behalf. Every community in the UK elects one person to represent them in the House of Commons. This person is called a *Member of Parliament*, or MP. Each community is called a *constituency*, and there are around 650 of them across the UK. Each constituency elects one MP, and so there are 650 MPs in the House of Commons. Everyone in the country lives in a constituency, which often groups several towns together. Do you know what yours is called?

We vote for who we want to be our MP at least every five years, on *General Election* day. On this day, everybody aged 18 and over goes to *polling stations* set up across the country, and puts an 'X' next to the candidate they want to be their MP. The candidate with the most votes in the constituency wins, and becomes MP for everybody in that community – even for the people who voted for somebody else. This 'winner takes all' system is called *First-Past-The-Post*; some people like it, and some people don't. Until somebody changes it, however, it is here to stay.

Most MPs belong to a *political party*, which I'm afraid is not as much fun as it sounds. A political party is a group of people who have similar views on how the country should be run. This means that when you vote for an MP, you are also voting for a political party. The party with the most elected MPs in the House of Commons forms the Government, and their leader becomes the Prime Minister. The Prime Minister is the head of the Government, or the *executive*, which runs the country. The Prime Minister lives at No 10 Downing Street. So you see, both Parliament and Government only have power because we, the people, give them power, which is why we call our system *Parliamentary democracy*.

What we mean when we say...

Legislature: another word for Parliament, which makes the country's laws. The legislature is made up of the House of Commons, the House of Lords and our Constitutional Monarch.

Executive: another word for Government, which uses the laws made by Parliament to run the country.

Parliamentary Democracy: the system in which people elect representatives to a Parliament to make laws.

General Election: the occasion when the country votes for the representatives who will become Members of Parliament. General elections happen at least every five years.

Constituency: one of 650 communities of voters within the UK, which elect an MP to represent them in Parliament.

MP: Member of Parliament. MPs represent the views of the people in their constituency.

Political Party: a group of people who have similar views on how the country should be run. We are going to look at the UK's main political parties shortly.

First-Past-The-Post: voting system in which the candidate with the most votes wins.

Debate and evaluate:

In a group, discuss:

1 The First-Past-The-Post voting system means that the MP with the most votes has to represent everyone in their constituency even if nearly half of the constituency voted for another candidate. Discuss whether you think this system is fair.

Read, research and decide:

1 Describe what happens in a General Election.

2 Explain in your own words the roles of the legislature and the executive.

3 Your MP represents you and everyone else who lives in your constituency. Carry out your own research to find out who your MP is and what political party they are a member of. Find out what kind of issues your MP has either supported or argued against. Do you agree with your MP's views?

CHAPTER 6: THE PALACE OF WESTMINSTER

The two main pieces of our Parliament jigsaw are the House of Commons and the House of Lords. It won't surprise you to hear that we call the place where they meet the *Houses of Parliament*, in London. Most people just call it Westminster, but its full, rather more impressive title is the Palace of Westminster.

Today, Westminster is the centre of political power in the UK. However, since 1998, Northern Ireland, Scotland and Wales have had their own Parliaments, or 'Assemblies'. This means that they have a little more freedom to make certain laws which apply to their own countries.

Royalty rarely visits the Palace of Westminster. In fact, our monarch only visits the Palace around once a year, to perform an important, elaborate ceremony called the State Opening of Parliament. As constitutional monarch, the Queen will process to the House of Lords' Chamber, where she gives a speech outlining the Government's plans for the year. The monarch's speech officially 'opens' Parliament for the year ahead.

The Houses of Parliament is an enormous place, with over 1000 rooms, 100 staircases, and three miles of winding passageways. Towering over the whole lot is the most famous clock tower in the world, and inside that, the most famous bell in the world: Big Ben.

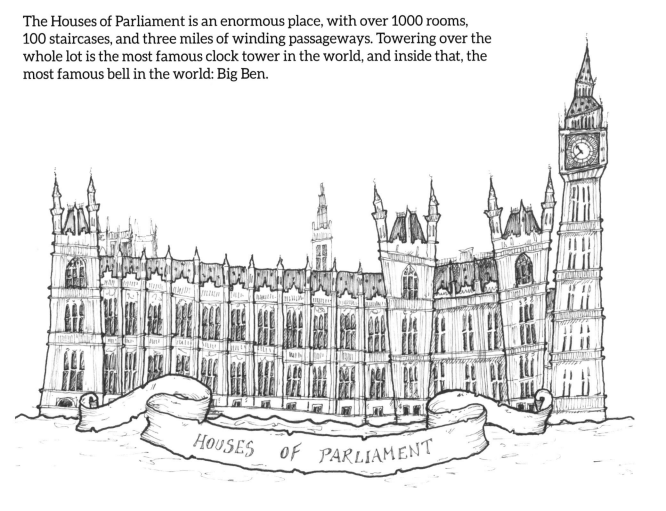

HOUSES OF PARLIAMENT

What we mean when we say...

The Houses of Parliament: the House of Commons and the House of Lords. They meet in separate chambers, and both are within the Palace of Westminster.

Big Ben: the nickname for the great bell of the clock at the north end of the Palace of Westminster.

Debate and evaluate:

In a group, discuss:

1   Why do you think that the monarch rarely visits the Houses of Parliament?

Read, research and decide:

www.parliament.uk provides an excellent research resource on the workings of Parliament.

1   Carry out your own research on the State Opening of Parliament and explain in your own words the purpose of this occasion and what happens on the day.

CHAPTER 7: THE HOUSE OF COMMONS

Over time the power of the House of Commons grew while the power of the monarch and the House of Lords decreased. Today, the House of Commons is the most important part of our democracy. This is a great example of the positive change you can make if you use your voice to stand up for what you think is right.

We have already seen how each community, or *constituency*, elects one person to represent them in the House of Commons, and that this person is called a Member of Parliament or MP.

Most MPs belong to a *political party*, and the political party with the most MPs forms the *Government*, which runs the country. All the MPs from the political party which forms the Government sit on one side of the House of Commons Chamber on green leather benches. It is important to remember that these MPs are *still part of the House of Commons*, and still help Parliament with its main job: *making the country's laws*. This includes the Prime Minister.

The only person who cannot be an MP is the monarch. In 1642, King Charles I stormed into the Commons to arrest five MPs for treason. Ever since 1642, no monarch has set foot inside the Commons Chamber.

The MPs from all the political parties that are not the Government sit on the opposite side of the Commons Chamber. These MPs are called the *Opposition*. The main job of the Opposition is to challenge the Government on how it is running the country. One example of this happening is every week during *Prime Minister's Question Time*, which you can watch online or on television.

Things can get pretty rowdy in the Commons when one side feels strongly that they are right and the other side is wrong. It is a good thing that people voice their views so passionately, but you might be surprised at how theatrical the whole thing sometimes is. In fact, some say that the two red lines on the floor separating one side from the other are just far enough apart that two drawn swords could not clash.

The *Speaker of the House of Commons* sits between the Government and the Opposition. It is the Speaker's job to keep the debates under control – a tough job, as you can imagine. MPs debate about everything from housing to hospitals to what the Government is spending our money on. After the debating comes the voting. One person from each political party tries to make sure all the MPs in that party all vote the same way. These people are called *whips*. MPs who disobey the whips are called rebels.

Before an idea becomes a law, it is called a *Bill*. A Bill goes through several stages of improvement from both the Commons and the House of Lords. Eventually, the Speaker announces the Bill for the final time, and all the MPs vote on whether they think the Bill should become law. If more MPs vote in support of the Bill than those who don't, then we have a *majority*. The Bill is then shown to the monarch, who gives it their *Royal Assent*. The Bill is now a new law, or *Act of Parliament*, and everyone in the country has to obey it.

So, let's sum up the four main jobs of the House of Commons:

- To pass laws (because it is the *legislature*).

- To say yay or nay to how the Government wants to spend the country's money.

- To make sure the Government is doing its job properly. This is called *scrutiny*.

- To discuss the many issues affecting the country, such as where our electricity and gas come from, or whether we should get involved in foreign conflicts.

What we mean when we say...

The House of Commons: the democratically elected part of Parliament. It is made up of 650 MPs, one from each constituency. The House of Commons plays the most important role in creating and making laws.

The Opposition: the MPs from the political party who have the second largest number of MPs. It is their job to challenge the Government on its decisions, and make sure the Government is doing its job properly.

Prime Minister's Question Time (also known as PMQ): a weekly opportunity for MPs to ask the Prime Minister questions. Prime Minister's Question Time takes place every Wednesday from 12 noon to 12.30pm when the House is sitting.

The Speaker of the House of Commons: the individual who sits in the middle of the Chamber and keeps everything under control.

Whips: people in political parties who try to make sure all the MPs in their party vote the same way.

Majority: the side that has the most votes.

Bill: the name for a proposed law, before it is voted on.

Royal Assent: the formal agreement of the monarch that a Bill should become a law. A monarch hasn't refused to give their Royal Assent since 1707.

Debate and evaluate:

1   As a class, listen to part of a Prime Minister's Question Time session. What are your impressions of PMQ? Do you think MPs ask fair questions? Were you impressed with the Prime Minister's answers?

2   Organise your own PM's Question Time. See if your Headteacher or their representative would give you a 'Head's Question Time' session so that you can ask questions about how they are running your school. In a group make a list of questions you would like to ask your Headteacher.

You can learn more about Prime Minister's Question Time on www.parliament.uk

Read, research and decide:

1   Write a paragraph explaining in your own words how Prime Minister's Question Time works. Do you think that PMQ is a good idea? Give reasons and examples to support your views.

2   Use www.parliament.uk to learn more about how a Bill becomes law. Using your own research write an account explaining how the process works. Explain what you think are the strengths and weaknesses of this process.

CHAPTER 8: COMMON INTERESTS – THE HOUSE OF LORDS

Unlike MPs, most members of the House of Lords are appointed rather than elected by voters.

To become a member of the House of Lords, firstly, you have to show how your experience in your career can benefit the lives of people all around the country. Secondly, you have to become really, really good at something. For example, it could be science, or politics, or law, or writing, or making money. The House of Lords is full of experts on everything you can imagine. These experts are very useful when it comes to making laws.

Remember, ideas for new laws are called *Bills*. Bills are mainly suggested by the Government, but can come from all sorts of different places. They could even come from you, if you feel very strongly about something and ask your MP about it.

The Lords cannot make Bills into laws because they are not democratically elected. Their main job is to scrutinise a Bill very closely and suggest improvements. Sometimes the House of Commons doesn't like the suggestions, so sends the Bill back again. And again. And again. The Bill goes back and forth between the House of Commons and the House of Lords until everyone feels that it is the best Bill it can possibly be. At this point the House of Commons votes on whether the Bill becomes a law.

The monarch appoints new members of the House of Lords, after the Prime Minister has suggested them.

After a short ceremony, they join around 800 members of the House of Lords, who all help to craft good new laws to help make the UK safer, happier, and fairer.

Members of the House of Lords are known as peers. There are three types of peer:

- You have peers who are appointed because of their special expertise in a particular area; these are called life peers.

- The second type of peer are the 26 Lords Spiritual; these are the Archbishop of Canterbury, the Archbishop of York and the Bishops of the Church of England.

- The final type of peer is a hereditary peer. Hereditary peers have inherited their position from their families. The vast majority of the House of Lords used to be hereditary peers; today, there are only 92.

A male peer is called a Lord and a female peer is called Lady or Baroness.

What we mean when we say...

The House of Lords: the non-democratically elected part of Parliament. Around 800 Lords scrutinise and try to improve the Bills suggested by the House of Commons.

Life Peer: a Lord or Baroness who has not inherited their title. They are usually an expert in a particular field.

Hereditary Peer: a Lord who has inherited their position from their family.

Lords Spiritual: the 26 bishops who sit in the House of Lords.

Lords Temporal: all the peers who are not Lords Spiritual.

Debate and evaluate:

In a group, discuss:

1 The House of Lords Act 1999 removed the entitlement of most of the hereditary peers to sit and vote in the House of Lords. Why do you think this change was made?

2 What do you think are the benefits of having experts from the House of Lords scrutinise, debate and suggest amendments to new laws?

Read, research and decide:

1 Carry out your own research on a member of the House of Lords. What is their area of expertise? Can you find any evidence to suggest they have made a valuable contribution to a debate?

2 Choose one of the hereditary peers sitting in the House of Lords. Do some research into their family and write a short account of what contributions their family has made over the generations to the history of this country.

CHAPTER 9: THE UK'S POLITICAL PARTIES

Unless a candidate in an election is an independent candidate, when you vote for your local MP you are also voting for a political party. A political party is a group of people who have similar views on how they feel the country should be run.

Before every election, each political party writes down their ideas for running the country in a document called a *manifesto*, which explains their *policies*. Policies are sets of ideas that each party would put into action if they won enough votes in the general election. For some years the two parties with the most MPs in the House of Commons have been the Conservative and Labour parties.

Here are some of the UK's political parties and their *ideologies*. An ideology is a system of beliefs and ideas:

- **Conservative Party:** generally believes in 'smaller Government'. This means that they think individuals should have more personal control than the Government does over the way in which they spend their money. They believe this benefits the country by encouraging *entrepreneurs* – people who set up their own business.
- **Labour Party:** generally believes in 'bigger Government'. This means that they think individuals should pay more *tax* in order to fund public services such as schools and hospitals that we all use. They believe this benefits the country by providing a more balanced society.
- **Liberal Democrats:** generally, this party is in between 'small Government' and 'big Government'. They emphasise the importance of personal freedom and tolerance.
- **UK Independence Party (UKIP):** thinks that the UK should be independent, and not part of a larger political and economic group.
- **Scottish National Party (SNP):** promotes Scotland's interests and independence.
- **Green Party:** promotes care for the environment and social justice.

When you are 18 years old, you can choose the party you think best matches your own views and vote for your local MP from that party in a general election. You can register to vote when you are 16. That's no excuse, however, not to start making your mark before then, as there are lots of ways you can participate in party politics at a young age. All the political parties are keen to attract younger members, and you can join in your teens. Joining means you will meet like-minded people, represent the voice of young people within the party, and campaign for the rights and interests of young people both within that party and beyond.

What we mean when we say...

Ideology: a system of ideas and ideals.

Manifesto: a public declaration of policy and aims.

Policy: a plan or a strategy.

Political Party: an organised group of people with similar political aims and opinions that seeks to get its candidates elected to public office.

Debate and evaluate:

In a group, discuss:

1 What is the benefit of having a number of different political parties to vote for?

2 The Green Party of England and Wales was established in 1990. Why do you think that new political parties are created?

Read, research and decide:

1 Carry out your own research to decide which political party you think you might support. Try to identify which policies you agree and disagree with.

2 Write a manifesto for a political party that you think should be forming the Government for this country for the next 10 years.

CHAPTER 10: DON'T BELIEVE EVERYTHING YOU READ – THE MEDIA

Have a think for a moment about how you know the things that you know. Some things you learn in books, like what the human skeleton looks like, or what happened in 1066. Some things your parents and teachers tell you. Some things you learn for yourself from personal experience, such as how ice cream sometimes gives you brain freeze. But how do people find out about what is happening right now, in their town, their country, or around the world? The answer is usually: *the media*.

Media is the name we give for the things that tell us the news: television, radio, newspapers – and of course, the Internet. The media gives us information about *current affairs*, everything from natural disasters and wars to celebrity gossip and sports results. It plays an incredibly powerful part in our lives, because it is responsible for a lot of our knowledge and opinions about the world around us and our place within it.

The media also tells us about the important things that are happening in politics. Examples might include details of a new law being passed, or information about a political party's *policies*. The relationship between the media and politicians is an odd one. The media relies on politicians for information, but it also forces politicians to be responsible for the decisions they make – what we call *accountability*. As consumers of news, our opinion on politicians and political parties is likely to be heavily influenced by what we are told by the media.

Newspapers are a very valuable part of our democracy, as they represent our right to freedom of speech without fear of Government interference. However, there is a popular phrase that you may or may not have heard. That phrase is 'don't believe everything you read in the newspapers'. This might seem like an odd thing to say; why wouldn't you believe what you read in the newspapers? Generally speaking, you can, but the phrase reminds us that since newspapers can print more or less whatever they like in this country, we should be aware that they can sometimes be *biased*, or unfair. A common example of newspapers being biased is when they clearly support one political party over another, and urge their readers to vote for that party at election time. Just like many organisations and individuals, newspapers have *agendas*, or motives, and it is well worth being aware of the difference between media that is biased and media that tries to be unbiased, neutral, or what we call *objective*.

Of course, people can reject what they read, hear and see in the media, and instead express their own opinions on blogs and social media sites like Twitter and Facebook. The Internet has dramatically changed the way in which we find out about what is happening in the political world. The good thing about this is that it gives people almost unlimited access to information, and allows political parties the chance to connect with people of all ages and backgrounds. But because absolutely anybody can post anything they like on the Internet, it also means that a lot of the information is biased, or simply incorrect. Again, it is a case of being aware of where the information you are reading has come from, and deciding whether this information is reliable.

It is incredibly important to be aware of what is going on in the political world. In order to use your voice effectively and make a difference to the things that matter to you, you have to know what is happening in the world. A good place to start would be the morning or evening news on the TV, or the politics section of the BBC website.

What we mean when we say...

Accountability: the state of being responsible for your actions.
Objective: not influenced by personal feelings or opinions.
Bias: prejudice for or against someone or something.
Neutral: not supporting or helping either side.
Agenda: an underlying plan.

Debate and evaluate:

In a group, discuss:

1 Make a list of the different ways and sources you use to find out what is happening in the world. How do you know that you can rely on these sources to be accurate?

2 The media is often critical of our political leaders. In what ways do you think this might be good for our society?

Read, research and decide:

1 Write a paragraph describing how you find out about the news. Do you read newspapers, watch the news on television or the Internet, or find out about stories on social media?

2 Describe which source of news you think is the most reliable. Why do you think this?

DO YOU REMEMBER?

Let's finish by reminding ourselves of some of the most important points we've learned:

- It is very important to be a critical thinker; this means being prepared to keep an open mind, take time to analyse and check the facts of a situation, consider more than one point of view and only then decide what you think.

- Democracy first came into being in Ancient Greece over 2500 years ago. A democracy is a country ruled by the people. A democratic system is one where everyone has a voice or a say in how things are managed.

- In Britain we have a democracy. The Government is elected by the people and, led by the Prime Minister, is there to run the country.

- Parliament is made up of the House of Lords and the House of Commons. Parliament makes laws, decides how the country's money is spent and scrutinises the actions of the Government to make sure the country is being properly run.

- In Britain our Human Rights are respected. Human Rights include the right to be safe from harm, the right to follow any religion (or none) and the right to speak freely.

- In Britain we have a constitutional monarchy; this is where the King or Queen acts as Head of State, but political power lies with an elected body such as a Parliament.

- The legislature in Britain is made up of the House of Commons, the House of Lords and the Constitutional Monarch.

- At least every five years we have a General Election to choose our MPs and our Government.

- It is very important to use your vote!

- Keeping up to date with the news is very important, but make sure you inform yourself from reliable sources of news.